Sam Rogers' Happiness Manifesto

This is a First Edition of the paperback
"Sam Rogers' Happiness Manifesto"
by Sam Rogers

Previously published as "The Happiness Manifesto"
by S.F.R.
As edited by Peter Michael Blackburn (without ISBN)

Copyright © May 2016 Tom Rogers & Carolyn Parry

ISBN: 978-1-910094-51-8

Published May 2016
By Magic Oxygen
www.MagicOxygen.co.uk
editor@MagicOxygen.co.uk

Printed by Lightning Source UK Ltd; committed to improving environmental performance by driving down emissions and reducing, reusing and recycling waste.

View their eco-policy at www.LightningSource.com

Set in 12pt Times New Roman

Title font: Merriweather

Cover original artwork by Tom Rogers

Cover design by Simon West

Contents

Dedication

To anyone looking for ways
to fulfil their human potential

Foreword:
Tom Rogers

Sam Rogers was my son. I find it hard to say this. I want to say he *is* my son but this could only be the case if consciousness continues after death. Even then, what meaning could the word son have outside this reality of flesh and blood that saw him born on January 5th 1989 at Queens Medical Centre, Nottingham, at 8:14 in the morning.

Even after having stood in that small room in the undertakers, staring at the lifeless body that bore a strong resemblance to a waxwork model of my own son, I did not quite believe that this was him. Whatever it was that I was looking at, my son's spirit was no longer there. I knew it was him. I said as much when I was asked to confirm that it was him, but at the same time this was just the scientific reality, that the cells that had grown to form those features, which were undoubtedly formed along the lines of the genetic blueprint known as Samuel Rogers, Sam to everyone that knew him.

It is strange writing a foreword to a book that is about being happy, and beginning by talking about death, but you can't get round it. The author of this book is no longer with us. He was a young man when he left. He would still be a young man if he were here now. Let me tell you something about him. I will not tell you much about him here and now. There is much that could be said but, this being a foreword to a book it must be brief and already it is not entirely that.

I would like to tell you about his childhood. I would like to tell you all about him and maybe one day it will be a more appropriate time.

For now, let's just say Sam Rogers was a philosophy graduate who tried to make a difference in the world. He did not merely study in order to get a philosophy degree, he studied philosophy in order to apply it and he did apply it.

The Happiness Manifesto is the thinking of a young man. It is his response to the state of the United Kingdom, even the world, as he saw it in the years following 2010 up until when it was first published and Sam, at his own expense stood outside banks in city centres around England holding placards carrying slogans such as "Dare To Imagine" or the enigmatic "Another way?" and gave away free copies of this little book to anyone who would talk with him. People did come and talk. They were inspired. Sam received emails from people who told him that this little book had changed their lives. At his funeral I was overwhelmed by hearing from so many people who had been touched by him.

Sam wanted to apply his skills to make a difference in the world. Sam believed in happiness as a philosophy and an attitude, not just a mood. He did not always have an easy life. He had much to contend with. The Happiness Manifesto was Sam's response to life and it was a gift to all of us. If you had met Sam you would know how charming and funny and witty he was, and you would have known what a generous spirit he had. You can feel that generosity of spirit in the pages of this book you hold. But you can also hear a young man's anger at some of the inhumanity that everyone is made to endure.

In response to unemployment, young philosophers being largely surplus to requirements these days, Sam trained as a TEFL teacher and went travelling in the Far East. He bought a motorbike and travelled a thousand miles across Vietnam on it. He got work in a Vietnamese school. He joined a Vietnamese football team. He was brave and adventurous and threw himself into the local culture.

Recently I was looking through Sam's journals from Vietnam. I was unable to look at them for a long time. Among many tales of this young man's adventures there were some reflections. "When I die" he said at one point "I want to be really living". Sam was really living when he died in a tragic accident in 2014.

When Sam gave away this book it was an act of charity. During his short life he had worked at festivals for Water Aid from time to time with his girl friend Jenna who was intending to join him in the Far East, where they were going to get married. Things did not entirely go to plan, but I think this reissue of Sam's book The Happiness Manifesto is a fitting tribute to a beautiful life. Sam's positivity and generosity of spirit touched everyone he met. No one else will have the privilege of meeting him, but in this little book you can begin to get an idea of the thoughtful, sensitive and adventurous man he had become by the time he was in his early twenties, and perhaps something of his spirit will touch you and you will be inspired to live with greater vigour and purpose and with a positive outlook.

The proceeds of this book go towards WaterAid. There is an horrific irony here, that Sam was killed by what he thought was a bottle of water. It was not.

Good clean water is essential to life. It was essential to Sam's life and it is essential to yours and mine. In many parts of the world there is no clean water available. WaterAid are aiming to remedy this situation. Buy this book. Help bring water to those who do not have something that should be a basic right, and perhaps you too will be inspired by the thoughts of a young adventurer. Maybe he will change your life as he changed so many while he was alive.

Alone in nature I play with light,
When the sun is a shining,
And all things are bright.
I try to make faces in all of the trees,
Out of varying hues,
Reflecting from leaves.

Shimmer and glimmer, dancing off of the river;
To me a cascading kaleidoscope delivered.
Casually skimming stones out of my hands,
I marvel at the ripples each time a stone lands.

Curling unfurling, smoke bends out my mouth,
Then meets with the breeze and journeys on south.
Try to hold on to a strand, twisting coercing,
As it drifts out of sight, as fully dispersing;
Into all that is past, and all that will be,
All that is you and all that is me.

The matter that makes up this universe,
Present in you from cradle to hearse.
And yet who fears death? Alas not me!
For I am part of all that you see.

Indeed how can I die, when fully aware,
That I am the sun, the sea, and the air.
When I know in a single blade of grass,
Lies both the keys to my future and my secrets past.
When I know with the beating of butterflies wings,
Each resonance caused is my soul as it sings.

Preface:
The Social Joke

Well you're curious and have made it this far, which pleases me no end. Curiosity may prove to be your greatest friend yet and its pursuit may in turn end up pleasing you a great deal. I hope this is so. Society and the social world we inhabit, as it currently stands, is something of a joke; so laugh. The great irony of the social joke is that what everyone fails to tell you is that everything's actually fine; or more precisely we have the capacity for it to be so. This capacity resides in your own self. You are brilliant. If for some bizarre reason you don't see that this is the case then it is because you have not yet allowed yourself to entertain the possibility that you might be.

I make no pretensions as to having all of the answers but want to encourage you to be sceptical and to consider the possibility that maybe no-one has all of the answers; or at least no-one has any answers better than your own. So what do you think? I seek to encourage you to pursue your own happiness and to consider the implications of this on a social scale.

As far as society goes, the sum of the whole is indeed greater than the sum of the parts; so what part will you play? Unfortunately our primary concern is our own preservation which at present is only achievable through the pursuit of money. But what will you allow yourself to be paid to do, and what are the moral implications of allowing yourself to be paid to do it? As our lives are still dictated by economic pursuit it would be nonsensical to suggest that you don't take this into account at all. However, there are many jobs that involve, or can involve, inhibiting your fellow man and conversely ways of enjoying your life and making some income as a result. I suggest that the latter is not only a happier pursuit but that the more we, as individuals, refuse to be the ones inhibiting our fellow man, the more that we will too become less inhibited as a result.

May we be the ones who say 'not in my name.'

So read on, but only on the condition that you want to. Boredom is one of humanities greatest crimes so I'm sorry if I've briefly incurred it. If I have then please pass this to someone who you believe may gain some pleasure from reading it. If you are still with me then maybe you want to consider where you are reading. Go to your 'happy place', take yourself away from today's questionably unnecessary necessities and place yourself somewhere where you are comfortable, receptive and capable of contemplation. We do so much and yet consider so little. Particularly, what our actions promote, imply and advocate. We will consider all this together, but first you simply need to be.

To Begin

With open ears, I have heard the whisperings of those who want change but know not how to achieve it. These same ears have also heard the first cries of those who are realising that freedom is free and that we can achieve change by changing one thing; ourselves. Your self and your own perceptions are the only thing over which you have full jurisdiction, so why not exercise it?

We are all products of society and expressions of an age and as such, ideas must always be understood in this context. Marx was right, at his time of writing, in recognising the proletariat as the majority class and thus in identifying their revolutionary potential. However, the language of the time is out-dated and no longer applicable to a modern society. Talk of clichéd revolutions (in the violent sense that we have traditionally understood the term), a deplorable means, is as laughable to an apathetic people as those who claim to be the oppressed proletariat when they are anything but. In truth, times have changed and ideas must develop with them. During recent governments, and particularly since the reign of Thatcher and her unfettered individualism, society has changed and we have all been sucked into the middle classes. Perhaps we should now accept these societal changes or at least accept that however we want to be perceived, the majority of us will fit into this socially constructed category. Individually you can choose not to identify yourself with a class as maybe, like me, you don't see it as any sort of reflection on who you are as an individual. Further to this, perhaps you would like to be recognised for the things that you decide are important to you; your friendships, your morality and not what car you drive or how much money you have; but what you choose to do with it.

At present British society, through its relentless pursuit of education, has produced an as yet unaccounted for generation that is too intelligent for the uses society would have for us. This generation is being priced out of a future and is disillusioned and hungry for genuine, tangible change. Daily witnessing hypocrisy, lies, false promises, contradictory and confused values, inequality and fear, this is a generation starting to notice and one from whom some are starting to think; no more. We see through this perfect system of division which renders us all unequal and binds us through its forever requiring maintenance. Furthermore we recognise the part that the media plays in inspiring us to hate those richer than us, despise those poorer than us and compete with those in a similar position. Talk of class may be used to try and divide us but we aren't a class, we are merely educated individuals who all have subtly different starting positions in a rat race we want no part in, and whose exuberant enjoyment of life and recognition of life's great potential is too great to be given up and exchanged for mediocre dreams that can be funded through mediocre labour.

Maybe, there are many other social constructs and ways of grouping people that, on consideration, we realise are laughable. The whole language of our politically correct current culture can be seen to be a backlash against the abhorrent intolerance of our past. However, legislation geared towards providing equality of opportunity merely serves to highlight, or more accurately, create differences between us. Perhaps what is more important is simply to treat people as 'ends in themselves', and you already have this within you. If you value your own happiness you will pursue your own goals and if, in fact, you realise that you do not want to devote your life to pushing pens to facilitate the endless movement of meaningless paper; you can make damn sure that you don't.

The development of modern capitalism has shown us the limitations of pursuing the compromise of equal opportunity through our failure to come even close to achieving this most meagre of goals. But why should we even set such compromised goals? Why are we trying, and yet obviously failing, to provide people with an equal chance to reset the balance of inequality in their favour? Aim for equality and achieve it through treating others as equal and ask as to why anyone would choose to run a system that does not. The idea that we need those who are in positions of power because we believe them to 'know better' is looking more and more ridiculous by the day, and in our current climate of 'economic crisis' it is fair to say that along with money, politicians have both outlived their use and outstayed their welcome. On paper it's all fucked but hang on a minute;

everything's fine. Are your basic material needs not met? The greatest thing modern capitalism has done for you is to provide the stability through which you are gifted choice. Capitalism can be hailed as getting us to the stage whereby, if we ignore our fundamental struggle and simply get on with it as many of us do, the biggest problems in our lives are our relationships with our friends and family and our struggle to be perceived as we want to be perceived by others, since as long as you keep up the day job you presumably have a roof over your head, heating, electrics and moderate comfort. Feelings of general alienation are perpetuated by the fundamental problems which seem to saturate our current existence and, in truth, could be easily overcome if we would but begin to tackle them. Indeed, who can feel any responsibility or accountability for their personal states when we must all battle to preserve our own, and when we deny ourselves any responsibility and accountability for the state of the world. As long as we continue to deny ourselves accountability we all take part in the theatre of global deception; stepping up on stage and acting our part in blaming everything but ourselves for the problems of the world and our own failings. However, global consciousness is shifting and the number of people who are starting to realise the difference they could make is growing. Through capitalism's creation of abundance we have got ourselves to the stage whereby we could have it all if we so wanted; and who could want otherwise? At present you have choice but it is limited within the framework of capitalism, within which your stability is only maintained through a constant struggle to keep your head above water. Real choice comes from the fundamental choice which many of us have not yet begun to consider; that of saying 'no'.

The system of economics which defines this current social reality is a human construct and a significantly flawed one at that. In the same way that we now find it absurd that it is only in the past century that both black people and women began to have their voices heard and their rights acknowledged, we will look back and laugh at the ridiculousness with which we allowed special printed paper to dominate our thoughts and keep us divided. You may ask what difference you make, but there is no doubt that you can. If for instance you want to live in a world where money doesn't matter then make sure money doesn't matter to you, and you've already achieved it for yourself if no-one else.

There are many of you out there already pursuing your own happiness but not yet seeing its wider social and moral implications, seeing it as a stop-gap, regretfully assuming that at some point you will have to 'grow up'. Recognise your social conditioning but refuse to allow yourself to be determined by it. I advocate, if you are not doing so already, considering what you want at all times. If you are not sure what you want to be doing with your life then start by doing what you want with your life in the immediate now, and the rest will fall into place. How could it not? In doing what you want you'll always be moving through time closer to being exactly where you want to be.

There is no doubt that we all have a moral compass so entrenched in our very being through social conditioning, however, we have hit a point now whereby, in the significant, and fundamentally significant most part, we no longer need rules of custom to tell us how to act and we feel patronised by them. In doing what you want you may discover that what you actually want is for others to be happy too, and for yourself to be directly and actively promoting and sharing this happiness with those around you, and to be morally accountable for your actions as a free-thinking individual. Furthermore, I will argue that the problematic personal state of feeling alienated from those around you or struggling to find meaning for yourself is perpetuated and upheld by institutions, bureaucracy and most crucially; money. Spend it when you have it and get by when you don't. You'll find you are able to do this and that in relying on money less, you will actually need it less. People get bogged down in the 'what-ifs' the second someone suggests the removal of money. How would it work, etc? It will work because we will have already made it work through not relying on money. Through making unwritten contracts of exchange amongst friends geared towards facilitating mutual material need, you can set the wheels in motion; moving us closer to a place where we'd be able to develop the intellectual maturity necessary to do things for each other without expectation of immediate return. Be generous and show yourself to value the happiness of other people over the current system's hailed means by which to attain it.

Still with me? Start small and deal with your immediate wants and desires and take enjoyment from doing so. Fancy a sandwich? If so what do you want in your sandwich? Make it happen.

On:

Being Happy

Quickly living
Slowly Dying
If I wasn't laughing
I'd be crying.

Derive happiness in the forever uncertain for it is all that can be known apart from contradiction. It is true that you don't know what tomorrow will bring, but it is up to you to be excited by this and to consider what you would like it to bring before making it happen. It is also true that if you didn't laugh at the state of the world you would surely cry; so laugh and do so wholeheartedly, provided you are doing the best you can to change the world within your capacity to do so. Every action you take changes the world. How it changes it and the extent to which you change it are entirely unknown, but consider how you would like to change it and what actions you will take once you know this to be true. Change but the way one person thinks and you've changed the world, so how do you want people to think? I'd suggest it should be for themselves. Take pride in your individuality for we are all the same and yet entirely different. I am not you and you are not me but I would seek to understand you as I seek to be understood. Don't judge that which you don't understand but always try to understand and take pleasure in doing so, even though full comprehension of another's perspective may never be entirely possible due to the fact that you weren't there and it was not your perception.

Smile. Or tell me why you are not smiling so I may try to rectify the situation. Smile at all you meet and who knows, someone may just smile back. Either way you haven't lost anything, but in each case you have so much to gain. Overcome people as strangers and see each person as a potential friend that you are yet to make. If someone does not want your friendship, then laugh in the knowledge that it is their loss, for you know yourself to be a good friend. If you are not a good friend, do you not want to be? Consider what this may mean for you and begin trying to make it happen.

Maybe you can save the world and maybe you can't; start by saving yourself. Love yourself. How can anyone else be expected to love you if you don't, and how can you begin to truly love others? If you don't love yourself then ask yourself, why not? Try and become the kind of person you could love and consider what kind of person that would be. By the same token, never lose sight of the present, for it is awash with opportunity. Stop thinking 'but what if?' and start thinking 'but what now?' as you move towards achieving the answers of the former question.

In embracing uncertainty you admit a lack of control, but this is the most empowering thing you can do, and through acceptance of uncertainty you may find you actually gain more control over your own reality than you ever dreamed possible. This being because, within your capacity to do so, you shape it. If you have decided that you are going to be happy, then be happy, and be defiantly happy if necessary and know that you will be fine whatever is thrown at you, and will continue to take the necessary action to remain so. Be happy regardless of what people think, be happy with and be happy without and see the bad things that happen to you as mere surpassable obstacles to your happiness as opposed to another excuse for you to not fulfil your potential. Don't let circumstance define you as it is not what happens to you that should define you, but how you react.

Live relentlessly in the present, for despite being ever-changing, it is the closest thing to certain that there is, for you can quantify it, rationalise it and crucially change it. Seize the day but do so at your leisure and only provided you know as to why you are seizing it. If you don't have reason to get up in the morning, then lie in until you do. The next sunrise will be all the more beautiful for it. All anyone can ask for is to die happy, and if you ensure your happiness at all times than you fear not death and why the hell should you? Who wants to live constantly looking over their shoulder and worrying about the future so as to miss the glorious bounty of the ever unfolding present? So many people are so afraid of death that they simply forget to live.

Let it happen and make it happen and watch serendipity become your reality. Start seeing the choice in everything you do. What you don't do is in many ways equally important as that which you do, if you have actively chosen not to do it. People think doing in itself is somehow worthy of praise, but if you don't know why you are doing what you are doing and if you actually don't really want to be doing it then I would suggest this is not the case at all. Pretensions to urgency are the hallmark of the self-important and laughable. What is so important in the grand scheme of things that the world would go to hell if you did not do it? And do you not want to be the kind of person who has time for people? You have forever and not a moment to lose.

Don't have regrets. They are simply a product of you not having done what you wanted to do in a given situation and avoidable if you always do as you wish. Smile knowing that if an opportunity has been unfortunately missed, there are millions more out there waiting for you and know that you'll be seizing the next one with both hands. And, know that you possibly only missed the last opportunity because you didn't truly want it. Do as you wish and say what you mean and don't accept any obstacle to your doing this. Accept no compromise on what you want and if an institution prevents you from achieving this, whether by making you speak in an unnecessarily inhuman manner, in a sincere yet insincere accordance with protocol, or even be it by making you adhere to a dress code that only exists so as to create uniformity and so as to not challenge people's perceptions; then question it. If on reflection you see these rules as a bit silly and repressive of your freedom to express yourself as you would like, then quit, and do so smiling. Accept no compromise because the little things do matter. Wake up the next day and think; what now? Consider the freedom you have and what you intend to do with it. Don't accept limitations on yourself or what you want; overcome them and in doing so overcome those of society also.

The root cause of unhappiness on a fundamental level is not being perceived as we want to be perceived, which can be seen as a direct result of us being unable to do as we please. There is a verbal aspect to this also in that we are frequently unable to say what we mean, or at least feel like this is so. Be articulate and take pleasure in language for through it you can better attempt to make yourself understood, and better attempt to understand and then facilitate the needs of others. One problem you may find is that the more you say, the less you say and the more convoluted your message. Fear not, however, be both articulate and clear, for the truth is so beautifully simple.

If you do what you want at all times you will be perceived as you want to be perceived for if seen, you will be seen doing precisely what you want to do. This does not necessarily mean you will be universally loved, but the people who matter to you will both love you and respect you, for if that is what you want, you will act in such a way so as to make it so. This does not mean doing what they want you to do, though what you want and what others want may often have correlation, and compromise between mutual interests can often be reached. In these instances you may find the compromise to be what you actually wanted due to its ability to satisfy mutual needs of which you may not have previously been aware.

What is life? We are life. You, I and all. Do you not love life? If not do you not want to love life? Indulge in people and you cannot help but love life. Invest in yourself and those around you and you can't help but invest in life and naturally in its promotion. Be Socratic and forever play devils advocate. Socrates' greatness was in his claiming to know nothing, yet constantly challenging, questioning and deconstructing the far less considered yet 'certain' knowledge of others. You may find you know a lot less in certain terms as a result but equally maybe much more. Less dangerous are those that seek true knowledge and seek to act morally than those who rigorously follow doctrines without question or without reflection. Win people with your laughter and share that of yourself in which you feel they may derive pleasure, whilst indulging them in that which sounds like their dreams. Question people and learn what you can about whatever they want to tell you so as you may better understand why they are as they are, what potentially divides you and how that may be overcome in light of yourself. May we stand together in our individuality recognising that which we have in common and that which we will no longer allow to keep us apart. Try not giving a fuck but caring deeply.

On:
Morality

Thou shall not park on double yellow lines
Thou shall not flaunt thy speeding fines
Thou shall not travel without a pass
Thou shall not walk upon the grass
Thou shall not dodge thy council tax
Thou shall not sit down and relax
Thou shall not teach without a degree
Thou shall not learn without paying a fee
Thou shall not first aid without a certificate
Thou shall not steal unless it's legitimate.

But who gave you power over me?
Who gave you the right of supreme deity?
Are you not too a human being?
Have you become numb to all that you're seeing?
Have you lost your senses?
For this makes none to me.
You stand in my way
And tell me I'm free.
That I am, but no thanks to you
So stand aside please,
I've got stuff to do.

As seasons pass, and years fall by, morality seems to have been cast adrift of the shores of modern life. I believe that we need to reconsider those things that make us moral, and contribute to a positive existence. Regain your autonomy and see your actions as prescriptive for if seen then they naturally, to some degree at least, are. How do you want to be seen and what do you want to be seen to hold as important? Be open but discerning. If you don't know enough about morality, make it your business to know enough as you should anything else. Learn and then laugh at the limitations of your borrowed knowledge, taking happiness in knowing yourself to be stronger for it. Knowledge and understanding of the limitations of your knowledge leads to a further openness to the ideas of others. We are, or at least should be, learning constantly; both through our own experience and those of others. If you are anything but dogmatic and militant in your beliefs but show yourself to be happy then more people will ask as to the source of your happiness and be interested to know what you think and why you think it. Many will be intrigued as to the source of your happiness, particularly if you are able to show yourself to be happy in the face of adversity, and to be happy with and equally happy without.

Wake up and start thinking about what matters to you. In promoting your own happiness you will naturally promote that of others for again; as social creatures our actions are, by nature, prescriptive. Furthermore it may be said that promoting your own happiness will naturally promote that of others, for what man or woman can be happy when what they believe is making them happy comes at another's expense? Love yourself, love people and follow your own happiness and you will naturally want others to do likewise and gain further pleasure in trying to facilitate and advocate that they do.

Question authority and be your own authority. Take pleasure in attempting to be moral; recognise yourself as imperfect but strive for perfection despite knowing that this may not be possible. Know that there is a significant difference between being moral and conforming to customary law. You are not necessarily being moral when you are simply maintaining the status quo, without any reflective time for genuine moral thought. If this is how you act, then all you are doing is regurgitating that which has been drilled into you over time, accepting that what exists is the playing arena within which you must perform and be judged. We delegate enough already without delegating to others what we should think or feel, and certainly without delegating to those men without a spine or a moral fibre in their body, let alone a personality; those whom we call politicians. Allow yourself to dream, consider how you want society to function and make that your reality through your treatment of others. Take pleasure in contradiction and be moral whilst defiantly being yourself and doing what you want. The only reason politicians, the police, bankers or anyone have any power is because of all those who allow them to have it. Take it back by empowering your self and exercising your freedom of will outside of institutions. So many people surrender their autonomy to the state and as a result let the state think for them. Think for yourself and decide what is important to you. Give the bare minimum to that which you believe to be a waste of time and the absolute maximum to that which you will, and refuse to let anyone else tell you what is and isn't a waste of time. In acting in line with, and so as trying to fulfil the obligations of others, you will always spectacularly fail because it is not what you want and your heart will never truly be in it. Even if you succeed in achieving someone else's projected goals for you, will it make you happy? I would suggest not. Use institutions and rely on them only to the extent that you have to and make that as little as possible. Instead make your life the most joyous expression of your own brilliant freedom.

Social contract theorists have defended the status quo by suggesting that we necessarily give up some liberty so as to protect ourselves from each other. I mean you no harm and what reason have you to wish me harm? It is because of repression, alienation, lack of meaning, lack of opportunity and equality and an inability to be perceived as we want to be perceived that crimes are committed. These evils are all the product of a failed economic system. Give people the freedom to do as they please and you'll find that they do not in fact want to hurt others, but want to love. It is only because we are not able to be honest and show love within this current system that many people don't, as they have not yet seen another way. Refuse to surrender your liberty and triumphantly claim it back for yourself and advocate it for all. I never signed the social contract and I do not consent to it. I consent to people and advocate you do the same.

Consent is crucial. I consent to you doing whatever you want. In fact, I implore you to and ask for you to afford me the same luxury, though I do not need your approval. It is through trust, honesty and consent that we must reclaim our autonomy, and together; our world. For example; murder and rape can be seen as morally wrong as by their very nature they violate the principle of consent. May the future be based on both honesty and consent. Surely the man who cheats on his wife is the greater villain than he who sleeps around but makes no pretence of doing otherwise? Everyone has different needs and different desires, and so there is no one-size-fits-all morality. It is through forever attempting to push one set of values and beliefs upon others that all conflict can be seen to stem from. Live and let live.

Theft is a grey area, for who so took the world from me and tried to sell it back? Take what you need and give what you can. Need only what you want and take only what you need, but consider what you want carefully, and what the moral implications are of the prescriptive action of taking it and whom or what you are taking it from. You may find, on consideration, that you don't want or need that much. Re-assert control over the things that society tries to take but which you can reclaim anytime you choose if you would but so will it; yourself, your freedom and your autonomy. If you are truly happy in yourself than it matters not what you have as you could be equally happy without it. Laugh at the greedy for they will never be truly happy for they forever require more and do so at the expense of others. I find it hard to believe that there are people, even within Britain, that struggle to put food on their tables and have to know what its like to be hungry and to know also that they do not have the means to be able to do anything about it. Well you do.

There is nothing wrong with materials but plenty wrong with materialism. This being because instead of seeking to provide the world with a service, you are seeking to make money and any service provided is essentially coincidental. In almost all cases corners are cut and false dreams are sold so as to make money at the expense of the individual. Attempt to redress this balance and do what you want whilst seeking to be a service to the world. Let enough money to facilitate your continued happiness be the resulting coincidence of such a service, and not the other way round, for as long as money continues to be the prevalent means of existence and beyond. I suggest that the more you and others do this then the quicker we can overcome money as the prevalent means of existence.

All is circumstantial. It is up to you to decide what is right in a given situation as there is no-one else viewing it from where you are standing. Know that it is through individual contributions to collective action that we can create a world representative of the new morality and global consciousness that is emerging.

On:
Politics

So, so long and farewell to you plotters and schemers,
A new age is dawning, an age for the dreamers.
So tired of being governed by the uninspired and small minded,
By money, ambition and greed they are blinded.
Trying to make my world as small as their own,
But my world is wide and I'm not alone.
Too stupid to see that as time is elapsing,
The systems by which they govern collapsing.
Of course they can't see a way out through the trees,
But I can for I can and will do as I please.

Sort out your own affairs before judging those of others and before thinking that you know anything so as to be able to prescribe it. I would not trust myself with power but I trust those who have sought it even less.

Can anyone truly represent you and do you need representing? I would suggest that the answer to both of these questions is no. Politics is everything and yet equally nothing, for it seems so far removed from our day to day life so as to be largely irrelevant, despite its claws reaching out to us through every bureaucratic piece of nonsense we must now seemingly conform to. I didn't want a Tory government as I don't subscribe to their values and policies, but I don't particularly want any other government either. Those in power only have power because we allow them to and because we acknowledge their power and their right to it. Deny them it and laugh at their attempts to exercise it.

Vote if you see it as your moral obligation to, if you want to and if you genuinely think it'll make a difference. But then consider the difference your vote actually makes and the fact that in voting you acknowledge the authority of the government and its subsequent actions. If their actions are ones that you do not want to be seen to be condoning, then don't vote at the next election. People suggest that in not voting and not exercising your political rights you lose the right to complain. Bollocks to that; you have more right to complain then anyone as you have chosen not to be represented and yet still there is someone claiming to be acting on your behalf. Do not complain, however, but derive happiness in knowing that change is possible and that it will be realised not through the current system's channels and means, but outside of them and through yourself, your ideas and how you act upon them.

The current government can barely claim to be representative of the people; let us further challenge the power they so flimsily wield by, at the next election, not voting for them and by not voting for anyone. Do this not because you don't believe yourself to know enough about politics to be able to make a decision, but because you do know enough and because you realise that you can't be represented and further more that you don't want to be represented. Some will claim that you have to vote so as to keep out extremists. But why compromise? I don't want extremists in power, but I don't believe anyone should be in power, so will not vote because I don't want to acknowledge anyone's right to power over myself or anyone else. I know that whoever is 'in power' will not affect me because I will make it so by not allowing them to affect me. In fact, the more extreme the government, the more defiant I will be in my happiness and in my laughter at their pathetic attempts to control my world. Refuse to be frustrated, refuse to be angry because in being either of these things you have allowed yourself to be affected. Smile because you are in control and because you know that the world you are trying to create and advocate is a better one; one based on love.

Capitalism is breaking and why are we trying to fix it? Because of all the good it has done? So we can maintain Third World debt? As long as we rely on the current economic system there will be poverty. Let us bring down that which allows us to rape a third of the world and then claim they owe us. A world whereby the banks lose half our money and then pay those responsible small fortunes while we are told we are poor, and run around worrying more about how we can maintain our now average existence.

We live in a target driven society and set ourselves meagre targets which we barely strive to attain. We pay people to look like they are trying to do things instead of creating the conditions where people are allowed to look after their interests and those of others freely. There's supposedly 1 billion hungry and world leaders agreed we were supposed to have halved that by sometime now- ish. But why are we paying people to find out who's hungry? And why are we paying people to draw up action plans which, until the fundamentals of the social world change, will never be realised? Maybe if instead of doing that we'd so much as provided a few extra 'sarnies' it would have been better use of a lot less money. Wouldn't the money that went into creating these pointless jobs have been better spent on food, on clean sanitation, on medical care, on provision of fresh water? In fact shouldn't we simply be giving people these things because they're actually dying, because up until now we have been depriving an absurd amount of people their basic human rights. Who runs this place?! Fuck beurocracy and fuck the numbers because they sure as hell don't add up. I stopped counting a long time ago.

It has also been quite some time since I stopped taking the papers too seriously. When I read the papers all I learn is who to hate and what to fear. I want to hate no-one and fear nothing, and do not want to know about that which is wrong with the world that I can't do anything about when I can consider that which is in front of me that I can do something about. Furthermore I don't want to waste my time working out who I should be blaming for my own limitations and who is such a cunt that I may excuse myself all my failings. The papers give a twisted morality that consists of cheering for one thing and booing for another, with little to no coherency. So who do you hate? The foreigners who supposedly come here and take our jobs or the unemployed who don't get them? The 'terrorist' throwing bombs back at 'our boys' who have been sent to do god knows what for god knows what purpose by idiots, or the asylum seekers who've fled so as to not have to face such madness. May we fight fear and stupidity with love and intelligence for they need no weapons to make a point. What's tomorrows headline? More good than bad happens every day. However if you condense all the sparse and isolated evils that happen across the world into an hour long show or an oversized pamphlet then of course it will inspire fear, enough that we deem governments necessary for the reactionary statements they can release and for the resultant propositions they offer. In doing so, they further legislate to infringe upon our liberty to protect us in light of what some very misguided individual may have done; invariably as a direct result of a life defined by the social conditions of inequality and oppression upheld by the very governments supposedly there to protect us.

And then, will you not laugh yourself silly when you realise that we could quite easily outnumber the very few. Those who genuinely have everything to lose because they have tied up their world in possessions of status, possessions that they have made exclusive at our expense so as to compensate for a complete lack of substance and a blindness to truth and beauty. And we aspire to these people? And we slave away for 5 out of 7 days so that we may have but a slice of their greed inspired luxuries? If it's that hard to maintain this embarrassment then why the hell are we still trying? And what will you do on the first day that you realise this? I thought sod this for a laugh, made a cup of tea, smiled to myself and began contemplating both my escape and yours. You are good and we are the people. Stop trying and start both being and doing in light of your potentially brilliant and all changing knowledge.

Britain is primed for revolution. Nothing will change and yet everything will change if we choose to change it. The great thing is, all you have to do is pretty much whatever you want. We politely say no all the time, so how about we simply change what it is that we are saying no to and let it be to institutions and denial as opposed to people. Whilst attempting to do so, hear your self utter the 'no' word only when necessary and preferably with a smile. This being on occasions whereby saying yes would infringe upon your liberty, your autonomy and your being perceived as you want to be perceived. Consequently, for occasions whereby you genuinely believe saying yes is not beneficial to the person asking. A truly British revolution by which all we have to do is politely say 'no thank you' to institutions and power save for people and theirs within themselves. Don't tell me I'm not a patriot, I want this country to be great, but I won't be proud until it is. I want us to create something so brilliant it promotes and advocates itself as opposed to forever trying to spread our own inadequacies. And promote it we shall for if we make a stand and lead by example we could be an inspiration and another major catalyst for further global change.

Unfortunately, like all other creatures on this planet, we are stuck in a constant battle to survive as we are still living in a system based on competition; and, in all competitions there are inevitably losers. Unlike other animals though, we have powers of communication, thought and empathy so great that we could easily overcome this if we only stopped competing. We think we're so clever and yet are forever foolish in allowing ourselves to remain the vicious animals we should no longer be. Our ruthlessness is disguised by being institutionalised into systems, which unless justifying genocide, we by and large accept and play our part in. This is something which if we are to genuinely start acting as if we are equal (which we all sincerely but laughably claim to believe) must be overcome. Freedom, equality, change. These are but words if not acted upon, and ones which politicians are forever bandying around. Well how exactly are you going to legislate for that? You don't know because it's impossible due to it being only possible if freely chosen by all. These are things we would surely all choose if we were freely allowed to choose them. Stop waiting for this day as it will never come. It is up to you to give yourself power by exercising it and using it to promote equality, change and the freedom of yourself and that of others. It seems to me that at present it's fuck or be fucked. Well fuck that 'cos I'm making love. Take pride and derive pleasure in your own expression and advocating of liberty. We have seen the results of a social economy based on competition; imagine what we could achieve if we actually began to co-operate. Ask yourself, do you want to be an animal living as a machine or a human fulfilling their potential? Stop competing and start co-operating with all but that which fails to encourage you to do so. You have nothing to lose but your mediocrity.

Question. Ask and you'll receive. Question, question, question and maybe, just maybe, you'll get some answers. However many you get simply depends on how many questions you're asking and whether or not you are asking the right questions. People do ask questions but fail to keep asking them so as to get to the fundamentals. Children ask why until you cannot give them an answer and I urge you to reignite your bonds with the child you once were who playfully did so. Knowledge is power, but what do you want to know and what will you do with the power you gain? Give yourself power by taking it back and by laughing in the face of those trying to deny you it. Next time someone tells you 'you can't', may you candidly inform them that you already have.

Red, blue, yellow... Mix them up and its all the same muddy brown. So long as we are still concerning ourselves with who should govern us as opposed to why anyone should be doing so then there will always be someone inadequately claiming to do so. While the grass may always appear greener on the other side and while the current Conservative-Liberal Democrat coalition (at time of writing in 2011) are a joke, I refuse to see Labour getting back into power as something to aspire to, something to have a song and dance about or as any sort of solution to sorting out the authoritarian pseudo-democratic, poverty stricken, debt-ridden mess that our country is becoming. Did they speak for you when they declared war on Iraq? I thought not. And do you think that people would mobilise themselves to kill people in far away lands if it wasn't for the fact that there is a body that seemingly has the right to do this? And would people sign up to do this do this if we didn't live in a system based on economics whereby again due to the need for our own preservation we must necessarily do things we don't want to do; selling ourselves to causes we don't believe in in exchange for our right to an average existence where we can almost afford enough of the things we're told that we want, that we allow ourselves to become content with bullshit, fear and mediocrity. Once again, I think perhaps not. Who kills people? Governments kill people and actively mobilise large groups of people to do so. Fuck politics, no- one should have that power. Why are we fighting anyone? We're a miniature island and there's no- one attacking us. Why are we playing world police when we can't even police our own streets, and yet they would not need policing if we all took social responsibility upon ourselves; something which would happen if only we were free to choose to. You are free to choose to.

May we free ourselves of all hypothetical imperatives and false obligations which we allow government and society to burden us with but which only work because of our own acceptance and compliance. Things are only significant if you choose to place significance upon them. So what's actually important? Society is the sum of its parts, but what part will you play? Try to be progressive of both thought and mind for as long as we concern ourselves with what everyone else is doing we will continue to stagnate at the lowest common denominator. So try being yourself or at least give yourself the opportunity to begin to find out what that might be. Stop listening to the self- interested grey preachers of compromise, the grim utilitarians so cold and calculating who dominate our times and listen to your self. The more you do the more you'll find that not only are you alright but potentially you are quite incredible.

On:
Religion

God is such an unknown hypothetical so as to not be worthy of consideration for fear of wasting one's time.

'God is dead and we are all his murderers.'

Alas, if only this were true. As with all the Gods of all the ages throughout human history; it is we who create them, we who destroy them and it is we who replace them with the ideas that are set to govern the next age of human existence. We may have slain the God of monotheism as the driving force of human action and understanding, but in its place gave rise to a God so sneaky that we don't even know we are worshipping it. A God that is as arbitrary as it is unfair and one for whom human sacrifices are made daily. This is a merciless God to whom we all devote the majority of our time but one who we could overcome as we have all previous Gods if we would but recognise it as our own creation and thus recognise also our power to destroy it. This is the final God who's destruction through rendering intellectually redundant would leave us to begin to understand ourselves as we are; humans, love and infinite potential.

Whether Jesus physically existed or not is again not really the point. He exists because he exists for many people as a core part of their ideas and conceptions on this reality, so it is this reality that must be addressed. Jesus would be embarrassed by the state of modern Christianity and by and large everything it has done over the past 2000 odd years. Stop being a Christian and be Christ-like. Did Jesus not feed a load of people with some bread and fish? Yesterday I fed six people with but a few eggs, some milk, some cheese and an onion; it's called an omelette and it was brilliant.

It is through attempting to institutionalise one man's expression of love and life that a very simple message has been lost. The Bible should have one word in it: love; with everything else as a footnote. The problem is that people unfortunately need it spelling out for them or allow themselves to think they do. You can see why the Ten Commandments, on a practical level anyway, came into existence. As a set of rules, their being obeyed has served so as to protect us from each other. Consider that we no longer need protecting. The Ten Commandments are a product of negative thinking and their being obeyed does serve so as to protect but it does nothing to help. Instead of considering what you can't do you should consider what you can do and further, what you actively will.

Do you believe in love? I do hope so. If you do it is because you have felt it, shown it, maybe you've actually been lucky enough to have received it. I love you or at least I love your potential. Just as the monetary system sees us forever buying back our own world, we are forever sold our own ideas by institutions. Religion removes the autonomous element from morality and makes motivation questionable. Think for yourself, hold beliefs but make them your own and be prepared to challenge and re-evaluate them. Refuse to give your morals away to a religion. If you agree, it is simply because the core ideas are your ideas anyway. Deny the usurpation of all by institutions. Believing in love doesn't make you a Christian; it makes you human. Revel in your own beautiful discovery and act on it.

Church, in so many ways, can be seen simply as a complete waste of time. Stop waiting for instruction and regain your autonomy and beliefs for yourself. Stop forever apologising for your limitations and overcome them. How can you achieve anything brilliant when you not only walk around feeling inferior and unworthy, but insist on constantly apologising for being so? The future is uncertain so don't waste your time living in fear of being judged but know you can justify yourself if called upon. If you can't then start acting in a way that would mean you could. So long as you clap your hands together and beg thin air to sort stuff out, nothing's ever going to get done. If there is a God he gave us liberty precisely so that we can exercise it to promote it for all and so that we may freely choose that which is good. Refuse to fix your nature for you are good and crucially you are more than capable of change; embrace it.

Whether you believe there is a God or not, do you or do you not, Christian or otherwise, agree with the sentiment of the Earth being given to us in common? I'd suggest you should and further that you should question anything that stops you acting as if this is the case. May we slay the false God of the modern age and resign it to history's graveyard.

On:

Work and Labour

Pass In and Pass Out

*Well, obviously you have to clock in somewhere
between these two vital stages;*

*Let the plastic box that is your master knows that you made it in
before the dreaded and punishable 9.01.*

Hell, these documents aren't going to stare vacantly at themselves.

Temperature, stable.

Adequate leg room provided.

*A 15 minute break every 2 hours to make sure your eyes don't fall out
of your head.*

Everything normal.

So why does it feel like I'm slowly dying?

*Like with the passing of each second and each moment I am aware
that it is a second that is lost and that I will never reclaim.*

*A fundamental awareness of the pointlessness and meaninglessness of
the tasks I must perform probably doesn't help.*

Neither does the profound realisation that in each moment I am not living, I am in fact surely dying.

But stay calm, panic not; there is no need to call an ambulance for the death of the soul is a slow process who's chief agent is boredom.

Boredom being such an inhuman state that it cannot be called a feeling;

It is an absence of feeling that many of us subject ourselves to in these sterile prisons of our own choosing.

The asylums for the sane.

Well excuse me if prefer to think of it as some bizarre, collective madness.

Yesterday I was so bored that my soul left my body.

I rose up out of my chair and levitated, slowly rising higher and higher as I began to rotate.

Quicker and quicker I span until, having stopped my upwards trajectory just short of the ceiling, the tension snapped and I shot up through that very ceiling of the office basement in which we dwelled.

Arms spread in Christ-like pose and with fury and bliss reconciled in their opposing of all that is dull I smashed on through floor after floor of endless nothing being tended to by the human doings.

Through desks and monitors I crashed and smashed though no-one seemed to take much notice.

Hell, they hadn't even noticed I'd gone and on they all typed and copied and projected; though their projections bore nothing of a human soul, unlike mine which finally burst out through the final ceiling and into the glorious day.

For the first time I flew and knew what it was to soar.

Up, up, up I soared until it was hard to believe that all the irrelevance of the targets being chased between 9 & 5 from Monday to Friday, being acted out in countless rooms in the countless buildings spread beneath me, were in fact anything close to the true reality and I relearnt the forgotten knowledge that it is not.

Away I thought and sought the free movement of water and the beauty of the natural world.

I spread my wings and dived down towards the river pulling up just in time to feel the spray splashing up off of the surface of the running water and over my once pallid, now sun-kissed face.

Today I flew again, but with body and soul perfectly aligned aviation was not necessary.

Having spent the morning dying I decided to spend the afternoon, and quite possibly the rest of my life, living.

Being unable to bend my mind to perform the quite simple requirements of processing the pages of nothing before me I had begun to feel stupid, which was strange for I knew that I was not.

In reaction to this I did something intelligent and for the second time in two days I flew.

I wrote a note, grabbed my coat and smiling walked out to be greeted by the sunshine that on a winter's day would've been missed entire.

I did not look back.

We feel alienated from our very selves in the modern day workplace as we are forced to pretend to enjoy having a crap time for little return, and to care about that which is in no way important to us whilst worrying about how we are going to continue to make our way through the hoops that we are seemingly destined to try and jump through until we collapse. We hear ourselves routinely and necessarily saying words in which we have no conviction and hate ourselves for it. And for what? Just as we must stop allowing politicians to act on our behalf, we must stop acting and speaking on behalf of companies if we are to regain our freedom as individuals. It is time for us to act on our own behalf for the benefit of all. Time for us to stop wasting each other's. Time we stop forcing people to struggle instead of helping them to thrive.

If you have a job, have a worthwhile job; worthwhile being however you define it. If your job is not worthwhile then maybe you want to consider as to why you are doing it. And, if you so much as consider it to be a job, maybe you want to further consider as to what you are doing it for, as should not all be at your leisure? Your means of maintaining an existence are not necessarily mutually exclusive with having a worthwhile existence, but in many cases under the current economics based construction of society, they are. If you don't have a job let it be because you don't want a job or because you don't want any of the options that are seemingly on offer at present. If you can honestly justify it to yourself then you can honestly justify it to others. If they don't like it, then that is unfortunate but symptomatic of a dismissal of an honest attempt to be understood due to an adherence to protocol and a morality stemming from economics as opposed to one based on people. As already discussed, such a morality is a selfish one. This being because at present services are not being provided due to some innate wish for others to be able to enjoy that which they can produce. Further to this it may be said that many forms of labour are no longer services at all; making the idea of doing such jobs existing as something which is somehow morally better than you're not doing them seem, quite frankly, ridiculous.

Even if you believe yourself to be genuinely trying to provide for people through the work you choose to engage in; how is anyone else to know so long as you have to charge for it to maintain your existence? Does this not annoy you? Would you not rather you could facilitate the needs of others within your capacity to do so through the things you enjoy and want to do and have your needs met through others doing likewise? Well, don't be annoyed for all is possible and together we can create genuine change. Not 'the big society' being given from the top down, whereby despite rising living costs we should volunteer to run our own public services for free, but the only kind of change that can ever truly make a difference... from the bottom, up.

Never allow yourself to be heard proclaiming the phrase which has become the ultimate get out clause of the modern age, 'It's just my job'. And if you do hear yourself utter such words; stop, think and be embarrassed as if you had just farted loudly at a dinner party, for adherence to rules that are potentially nonsensical is far greater an offence. Denying yourself accountability for your actions on the grounds of something just being your job is ridiculous, embarrassing and also potentially very dangerous, for how many of your actions are there then that are unconsidered and not your responsibility? Are you but a machine? And is it because deep down you know that your job is an irrelevance that you insist on trying to get some power through denying another, in an attempt to compensate for the fact that you are powerless because you forever deny yourself? Stop denying yourself and stop denying others and regain power through your rejection of its necessary existence outside of yourself.

Another phrase which will forever amuse me on utterance is 'I'm afraid it doesn't work like that'. Well tell me how it does work then and then tell me why it works like that? If the answer is love then fair enough but if the answer is 'because it doesn't' then I suggest you may want to consider why that is the case. If you are unable to give a reason then you essentially don't know why you are doing what ever it is that you so routinely do, and I suggest if viable that you quit and do something that you have conviction in. Are you a human being or a human doing? Regain your purpose in knowing precisely why all your actions are so and let that be because you are driven by your own happiness and freedom and because you know your pursuit of both will not only bring you both, but maybe even make it possible for all.

Don't do jobs that require you to behave in this manner and don't just do your job if the resultant actions mean condemning yourself to not being a person. Don't be a parking officer, don't work for border control, don't be a taxman, don't work in insurance, don't work in a call centre where people who don't want to be there phone people who don't want to be disturbed, and, dare I say it, and while for many of you your intentions will be both honourable and admirable; if you care about justice don't be a policeman, be just. If you care about your country don't be in the army, for who so threatens us that we would want to threaten them, and who are we to profess that we know better when we fail to cast our eyes over the amusement that is our own supposed democracy?

If we must talk of class, a lamentable and dividing social construct caused by the inequality inherent in capitalism but a topic which is never the less unavoidable when considering the history and make up of work and labour, then I will say the following...

It is hard for the true working poor to be revolutionary for they do not have a moment to question their condition and do not have the necessary surplus that creates choice. Due to inequality of opportunity they are necessarily consumed by simply trying to meet their basic material needs and provide for their families. However, the rest of society owes you, for it is you who physically builds and maintains all that depicts how man has so profoundly shown its capacity to shape, and continue to shape, the world like no other creature on this planet. Conversely it is the middle classes, who have greater choice, who for too long have intellectually supported stupidity through their compliance. They have allowed others to languish in total poverty for fear of losing their own moderate comfort and being resigned to the same fate, and have lived in the false aspirational hope that one day they may join the elite who ensure that total poverty prevails. This can continue no longer if the sickening concepts of class and that which upholds it are to be overcome. May we start by realising that already the old notions of class are dead. In truth there is now only the 1% who live at everyone else's expense and the rest of us who uphold this. It is now up to us to acknowledge this fact and begin to consider what we can do both together and as individuals to overcome it.

Whatever privilege you have, it is pretty much your duty to abuse it so as others may do likewise. You can only act within your capacity to do so, but I urge you to consider that for many of you this capacity is greater than you think. You have an obligation to yourself to make sure your basic material needs are met and, as in the world as it stands this will not necessarily be done for you; this is your primary concern. Once this is achieved however, what will you do with your surplus and how much surplus do you need? If we must lose some luxury so that the basic needs of others are met then so what? Should not the basic needs of others be the most basic of our aims? And, in reality, in Britain these basic needs wouldn't even be that basic as we could all have luxuries that are often taken for granted; hot water, gas, electricity, modes of transport, phone lines, the internet, and anything you need or care to mention could all be ours if instead of seeing their implementation as potential capital for ourselves, we saw them as services which by right should be available to all.

Consider what would happen if supermarkets were made free to the public. Everyone would go mad for a week or so but then realise that they should only take what they need so that others may do the same. Further that in order for farmers to keep farming they must be afforded all the services they require and want so as to keep them farming so long as that is what they want to do. For this to happen all other services would have to follow suit and any service which isn't truly a service would be made redundant for it would not be contributing to the maintenance of the empire of the happy. The future is uncertain, but in knowing that from small changes big ones can result you will find strength and happiness in your ability to instigate change. You may not have the power to make supermarkets free, but think about what you can change because in reality that is but a small change but one that if imagined fully would have massive consequences.

Use your imagination. How would it work? The assumption is that everything's working right now but ask yourself, is it? It'll work because we will make it work and because we will have to. What's more, we will be driven by the recognition of our contribution to make it so pursued in our own way. Put your faith back in the only thing you can if this world is to be a better place: people. If shown trust and given responsibility, and what's more if that responsibility is free and self-chosen, they will show themselves to be worthy of both. We have seen the results of a 'planned economy' so let us try an unplanned one. In fact let us have no economy, save one of people.

Many of us struggle to find meaning in our labour because much of it is pointless and simply there to maintain the endless movement of that which keeps us divided. Meaning could be found in the most mundane of tasks if it were genuinely necessary, freely chosen, performed at your leisure and ultimately rewarding as part of your contribution to a happy society. How could this be so? All jobs would only exist because they are necessary and yet would not be jobs at all; merely contributions to shared responsibilities, freely chosen by individuals and performed at leisure. What if through education we were able to teach the importance of your freedom and how you choose to exercise it, so as to show how everything you want to do is only facilitated by others being allowed to do what they want to do and by their considering you and everyone else as part of that. Would that not give purpose? Would you not find motivation in the morning to get up and support that? And would it not ultimately make you happy?

Art and our potential to create and express is arguably that which truly separates us from animals, but something which falls by the wayside and becomes more and more difficult to actively pursue and achieve in our current construction of society. If we are to continue to produce works of greatness and beauty and the kinds of human achievement, attainment and fulfillment we should aspire to, then society must become truly free. How can the artist begin to create if he doesn't have the time as he must consume himself with enough paid but not necessarily (fundamentally) necessary work to maintain his existence. And then, in an age of file sharing (which wouldn't be bad at all if it wasn't for the fact that artists need money like anyone else at present), even if successful there are no financial guarantees. But music and art should be shared and enjoyed as should anything and everything else we can either create or provide.

No-one truly wants or dreams of being an insurance salesman or a taxman, so why allow yourself to become one? These jobs don't actually need doing; they only do so if we continue to care about money and its forever movement and management. So many jobs of this ilk could be happily scrapped. As long as people need money, they can be paid to do anything no matter how pointless. After its removal we would see what is truly important as people would have no more cause to pursue anything that is not. As we'll have got rid of meaningless jobs, yes there will be fewer jobs but as a result more time for pursuit of the arts. Why are we so afraid of making life easier for ourselves? Do less and be more. If you can't be creative in your job, be creative without it if it is possible for you to choose this. I'm creative and you're creative. The only reason you may not be is if you haven't yet tried being creative or seemingly haven't been afforded the opportunity to be. Afford it to yourself. Be creative and see what you can create. May it be a better world.

Epilogue

So let me make this clear, there's a choice to be made;
Choose to live or choose to be paid.
With the former who knows just what you might do,
The latter's already laid out for you.

Now about this latter of which I speak,
You'll need to be working five times a week
And while this may sound a little mundane,
Once a year you could have a week in Spain.
Off the Costa del Sol though yours will be gone,
But who cares, grab a beer and get your tan on!

In the evenings you won't want to stay up late,
As you need to be out by a quarter past eight.
So fall into the sofa, whack on the TV.
Britain's Got Talent, now in HD!

At the weekend get smashed in shitty chain bars,
Where tangerines are impressed by men with cars.
So save up for one as you'll need a wife,
To compromise with for the rest of your life.
Together get a house as that's what you do
And decide the shades of beige that'll best reflect you.

The work cycle continues 'til you're 65,
By which point you may have forgotten; you're alive!
Your youth may be gone but look at the amount,
Tucked away in your bank account!
No amount can buy back the time that you've lost,
You may have possessions but at what cost?

And when you realise that you've wasted your life,
When you realise that you don't love your wife.
Will you not spare a little thought for me,
When I told you you're the master of your own reality?

For the truth of your existence will be made true,
By everything that you choose to do.
So money or time, what's it to be?
Money or life?
Determined or free?
For there's a choice to be made in case you forgot,
Money? Hmmm, I thought not.

Through capitalism we must necessarily keep consuming our world until we destroy it. The world existed long before us and will continue to exist long after us. The question of whether it has value in continued existence due to no-one being around to perceive it is another matter. If we want to save the world, we are talking about our world. The conditions in which this is possible are only possible in a society whereby we are all free to choose it. We'd all have solar panels on our roof if we didn't have to pay for it, just like more people would go to the Third World and help build houses and create the infrastructure necessary for self sufficiency if they didn't have to pay for it and suffer in return. Because all is money; even green energy and charity are driven by business and as such the causes will always be secondary to economic necessity, and unfortunately also potential greed. At some point the universe will dispense of us, but let us not dispense of ourselves. Money creates inequality, and moving away from it is the only way such conditions could be created within society whereby we can ensure not only the continued survival of human beings but also their continued happiness.

Everything denying us appears as but a minor inconvenience that makes up part of the apparent 'have to-s' of day to day life. Because they are seemingly only minor we tend to accept them, albeit with a grumble, but how many will you suffer before you realise you are barely able to do anything that you want to do freely and at what point will you say 'no more'? Start doing what you want and start now. When was the last time you took a bath? I don't mind showers but at the same time often resent them for my taking one usually means I haven't had time to take a bath. Now I've mentioned it do you feel like taking one? If so how do you want it to be? Consider what kind of beverage you might want to take in there. Maybe you want to think about what album you're going to put on, what nice smelling soap stuffs you're going to wash with and how many candles you're going to have. And hey, who knows, you may even want something to read in there. Luckily the latter's already sorted for you.

As yet we have nothing to lose, so let us be careful what we gain until we have set up the conditions whereby we can together claim it all. Never become too stable in anything other than your continual happiness. This shall be your greatest strength, and makes you rich regardless of property or wealth, and renders you capable of dealing with whatever the uncertain future throws at you. This is because what is certain is that you'll be doing what you want and that this will make you happy, and because what you want to do will involve actions geared towards creating and facilitating a future whereby you and others alike are free to continue doing that which you want to do and that which you will.

Don't worry, you're probably fine. Worrying is the most pointless of undertakings and often most indulged in by those who don't truly have much to worry about. If you are in debt, which most of us are now, then what the hell does that really mean or matter so long as there's a roof over your head and food in your belly? I don't believe in saving money as I don't believe it to be compatible with saving people or saving this world, and as such I would rather see it drown or burn. If we are to sort out the environment and the third world, then we must move away from money as we cannot even begin to tackle these issues seriously so long as it is necessary for us to exploit the world to maintain ourselves individually. Show money the respect it deserves; none at all, but give people the utmost until they show themselves to not be worthy of it and even then show yourself to be capable of forgiveness and forever love the world. Don't count the pennies but forever keep the *change*.

May we fight our own placation. I thought the kind of revolution Marx speaks of would simply not be possible because of the extent to which we have been divided and forced to be individuals in terms of our primary concern being our own preservation. Also because in allowing us to have comfort, and in the creation of the middle classes, we have allowed ourselves to be placated in our moderate comfort and our struggle to preserve it. As such our generation, on the face of it, can be said to have very little to fight against or at least many of us don't yet realise that we have something to rail against because of this moderate comfort. Not only do we have much to stand against but more importantly we have something to stand for and much to live for. That being for everyone to have access to whatever privileges you have been fortunate enough to enjoy, and be free from all that has ever caused you hurt. There is no longer anything that unites us but our difference, so may we celebrate it and live out our existence our way whilst allowing others to do likewise and laughing at that which tries to stop us.

Is what we have truly worth fighting to preserve? Will you fight to preserve your freedom to struggle for mediocrity at the expense of both others and your very self? Or will you risk it for something more? The sky's the limit, and even that's only if you fail to allow yourself to entertain the possibility that there might be something beyond it. I, for one, would rather go blind from looking at the sun then staring at the TV.

You are unfortunately gravely mistaken if you believe us to be born both free and equal. We are not free as we are born into economic slavery and we are not equal as we seemingly all have different starting points and opportunities within that system of slavery. We are now a people born into debt, but may we be clear in stating that we have a right to life, that we owe no-one for our existence and that we will not be priced out of a life and a future. May we be the ones who do that which previous generations have failed to achieve as they forgot their youth and compromised on their own future and ours. May our children be both that which they ought; may they be born free and equal and may we proudly say that out of love we fought to achieve this for them.

There will not be a revolution in the way revolutions have happened in the past and in the way we currently conceive of them, but potentially there could be an infinite and unknowable number of personal revolutions that together could shape the world and the future. What do you want to do? What are you good at and what is your dream? Do whatever you can within your powers to achieve it and if you do not yet know that which you will, then worry not, but do as you please while you consider what it will be that will please you entire. I am inspired by what I could do if I but let myself. You should be too. The only person who can grant your freedom is yourself, so advocate it and promote it through the prescriptive nature of being seen to exercise it. Whatever happens; hey, you're going to be happy and your happiness will naturally and necessarily encourage the promotion of the creation and maintenance of a society in which we could all be happy for you wouldn't be happy if it did not. There are many questions we should be asking, but know that the answer is you and derive happiness from this fact so long as you are justifying that claim.

Delegation in labour and in who runs this place has for too long relieved us of responsibility, but let us be responsible. If not you then who else will? It is true that in the current construction of society it is hard to make a difference; but that's only so long as you go along with it. If you want to make a difference then do something different and support others trying to do likewise. If you don't agree with a company's morals, construction or that which they uphold, then don't work for them as while their doings may not be directly your fault, and while they may be able to offer you enough money to just about attain the middle class dream, simply going along with it suggests that you think that's all fine. See the prescriptive nature of that which you subscribe to, and be careful what you allow yourself to advocate through compliance. If you can't afford to do otherwise then you are relieved of any moral responsibility, but if you can then I suggest you consider the power you have. There have been loads of jobs lost thanks to those who we have allowed to profess to know best, but maybe it's time to be your own boss. Don't allow yourself to be humiliated in being made redundant, but quit and make yourself useful. If you feasibly have that capacity I suggest you may derive happiness in it. What will you do and what will you stand for? I can usually take even the pit falls of my actions with a smile for at least they are my own. In that sense I'm happy, which poses a few questions. Who's going to stop me, and why would you want to, for I'm certainly not stopping you? Who are you going to allow to stop you? Let it at least not be yourself.

We stand at a crossroads and the choice is ours to make. We must either record all we do or record nothing. We must either keep fighting crime, a losing battle so long as we keep making more and more a criminal activity by legislation, or remove law and watch as there are no crimes. Some among us through inequality of opportunity are condemned to crime before birth, and we are all guilty of the real crime of allowing this. Equality is everyone having the same level of support and the same level of reward. That being access to whatever they want or need to make and continue to make the contribution they want to make to be part of a world in which that's possible. Instead of unequal opportunity to attain a new equilibrium of inequality in which we may have a slightly higher standing, should we not be striving for this total equality, the equal opportunity to be different and the maintaining of a society in which this is possible? I am too intelligent to do most of what is set before us and so are you so long as you refuse to allow yourself to be insulted by doing it.

Change is coming if you want it, and if you realise that this is what you want you can accelerate it by considering what your part in glorious revolution will be, and by taking pleasure in realising it. We've paid into pensions for no return; we've trusted our money to banks and watched them go bankrupt. We've surrendered our liberty and delegated to people who have taken us to wars without our consent. We have removed the creative element of almost all labour and created a world in which the majority of people are struggling to merely stay afloat. Well build yourself a massive raft. Take off the stabilisers and find you can ride your bike perfectly well and always could. You have a choice to make... You can deny yourself responsibility and accountability for the state of the world like everyone else, or do something different and take on both with a smile and find meaning in your contribution towards another way. I don't know what your expression of truth and beauty will be but make it true and beautiful.

So what are you going to do tomorrow?

Dare to imagine.

From:
The Author

I'm forever losing and finding things including myself. It is when I am doing what I want and being as I wish and when the outcome of this is the increased happiness of others, that I find myself and at these times that I feel most alive. When I do lose myself I withdraw but oh so slightly, quietly confident in my wait to find my new equilibrium in an ever changing world, knowing that the only way is up because I will make it so, and that life would not really be worth living if I thought or did otherwise.

My existence over this past year has been so entrenched with that of which I speak that it has become inseparable. I allowed for the possibility that I may have almost nothing, and you gave me almost everything and certainly more than I would've ever asked for. And no, I don't always get it right but it's okay so long as I feel like I can honestly say to myself that I'm trying and so long as I am I'm happy. I could never recite this text word for word but if we met I'm sure we could find something on which we agree, and to some degree I think you'd understand.

May we have an uprising of love and freedom of expression. There will be no guns and there will be no violence, for nothing worth spreading requires them. You are good at something though you may have not given yourself time to find out what that is yet. However there is a contribution you can make towards a better world that no-one else can, and I hope that what I'm good at is helping you to realise this. Your world is THE world; make that better and together we may create a better world for all. Our numbers are growing as we begin to stand both alone and together for what we believe. Do something different today and start asking why.

To anyone who picked me up over the summer when I was hitch-hiking without a working wallet or phone, from the long term MS sufferer turned heroin addict and his ex heroin addict mate who looks after him who drove me for 5 and a half hours from Sheffield to Edinburgh and constantly plied me with coffee and cigarettes, for being true good Samaritans; to the car in front of the 'skagheads' in a dog collar who drove straight past looking away for showing me the amusing nature of his 'faith'. To everyone who said yes to me for being open and somehow brilliant in their own way for taking a risk and doing something different, to everyone who said no for making me laugh in the knowledge that they mainly deny themselves and for spurring me on. To all my friends and family who repeatedly greeted me after long days and many miles with hot food and a bed, or a beer and floor space and always oh so much more. To the boys at 30 Flora who gave me a room from which me and another dear friend were able to live out our intended 'summer of love'.

To Jenna Cousins for being so loving and supportive of me over this past year.

To all of you; *thank you.*

I'm Samuel Francis Rogers... Who are you and what will you allow yourself or decide to become?

thehappinessmanifesto.blogspot.co.uk

About:
WaterAid

In support of
WaterAid

WaterAid's mission is to transform the lives of the world's poorest and most marginalised people by improving access to safe water, toilets and hygiene.

These human rights help improve health and break the cycle of poverty.

We work with communities, local partner organisations and governments to make change happen, from installing simple technologies to changing national policies.

Our vision is of a world where everyone everywhere has access to safe water, toilets and hygiene by 2030 – help us make this a reality.

**To donate funds directly to WaterAid
in memory of Sam Rogers
please visit JustGiving.com/Thomas-Rogers1**

About:

Magic Oxygen

As well as publishing a wide variety of books, Magic Oxygen also run a series of writing contests. The main one is the Magic Oxygen Literary Prize, fondly known as MOLP, which has a £3,000 prize fund and takes the winners into print. Additionally, the Mini-MOLPs are diverse writing contests with thought provoking themes inspired by international environmental awareness events.

These writing competitions are unique because Magic Oxygen plant a tree for every entry received in their Word Forest in Bore, Kenya; they even send the entrants the GPS coordinates of their trees. Their contests also funded the construction of an urgently needed classroom at Kundeni Primary School in the same community. The new classroom was officially opened in May 2016 and work has started on building the next one.

This pioneering reforestation and building project is carefully coordinated by forestry expert, Ru Hartwell of Community Carbon Link. He chose Kenya to site the tropical Word Forest, because trees planted near the equator are the most efficient at capturing carbon from the atmosphere and keeping the planet cool. Ru picked Bore because it's a remote community that had suffered greatly from deforestation. The newly planted saplings will eventually reintroduce biodiversity, provide food, medicine and water purifiers, and they'll also create an income stream for the community too.

You can play a vital role in this legacy project by buying a block of trees and building materials - visit MagicOxygen.co.uk for further details.

Mini-MOLP June 2016:
Sonnet for the Solstice - 14 lines

Wax lyrical with a Shakespearian style sonnet and
imagine it performed at the break of day on the solstice.

*Take inspiration from **World Environment Day** or **World Oceans Day***

Mini-MOLP July 2016:
Postcard from the Park - 200 words

Pen a postcard-sized piece to anyone or anything,
with your arboreal thoughts and stories.

*Take inspiration from **National Parks Week** or **National Tree Day***

Mini-MOLP August 2016:
Last Words Monologue - 400 words

The film is about to end, the last of a species is about to die.
Write the script of their parting words.

*Take inspiration from **World Honey Bee Day** or **World Elephant Day***

Lightning Source UK Ltd.
Milton Keynes UK
UKOW05f0732010217
293347UK00009B/189/P